20 Answers

Mary

Tim Staples

Catholic
Answers
Press

20 Answers: Mary

Tim Staples

© 2015 Catholic Answers

Published by Catholic Answers, Inc.

2020 Gillespie Way

El Cajon, California 92020

1-888-291-8000 orders

619-387-0042 fax

catholic.com

Printed in the United States of America

978-1-941663-68-4

978-1-941663-69-1 Kindle

978-1-941663-70-7 ePub

Introduction

The special reverence that Catholics give to Mary, the mother of Jesus, is one of the distinguishing marks of Catholicism. But this devotion to Mary is not just a nice little Catholic add-on—it should be an essential part of belief and worship for *all* Christians.

There are at least two reasons this is so. The first is rooted in the Fourth Commandment: "Honor your father and mother." If Mary is the mother of Jesus, and Christians are Jesus' brothers and sisters, we are required by God's command to honor her as he does.

Second, by saying "yes" in Luke 1:38—"Let it be done to me according to your word"—Mary helped bring salvation to the whole world through her son Jesus. How can we respond to so great a gift other than to offer her our gratitude and our praise? Prophetically speaking, the inspired Psalmist sums up our thoughts powerfully in Psalm 45:17:

> I will cause your name to be celebrated in all generations; therefore the peoples will praise you forever and ever.

Theologically speaking, it's vitally important to understand the truth about Mary because of what it means about Christ. For example, if someone denies Mary is the Mother of God, the question becomes,

"Who, then, is Jesus Christ?" Jesus necessarily becomes either a mere man, or two different persons (one divine, one human), or else not a person at all but some sort of amorphous and unknowable *thing*.

Correct doctrine about Mary eliminates the confusion, and points us to correct doctrine about Jesus.

Marian doctrine also points to truths about who we are as human beings. The Immaculate Conception, for example, reveals to us the dignity of the human person and how God gives grace to men in order for them to be able to accomplish things far beyond human nature's ability. Learning about Mary aids in the discovery of the nature of true greatness in the body of Christ and the accompanying honor that is due to its members.

In this booklet we will explore Catholic teachings about Mary, show how they're rooted in the Bible and ancient Christian belief, and contemplate with joy what they mean for us as Mary's spiritual children.

1. Who is "Mary of Nazareth"?

Though she became the most famous woman in the history of the world, Mary was born a simple Jewish girl from a poor family in the house of David,[1] some 2,000 years ago. When she was fourteen or fifteen years old, God chose her to be the mother of Jesus Christ, God incarnate; this simple teenage girl then became *the Mother of God.*[2] She was, as a matter of history, called to the unique task of bringing the Messiah into the world.

Mary is a sign to us all of how God loves to choose "what is weak in the world to shame the strong" (1 Cor. 1:27).

Mary's life and identity are really all about her divine son, Jesus Christ. Her greatness, her holiness, in fact, anything of eternal value in her at all comes entirely through her relationship with him. In Mary's words, "All generations will call me blessed; for he who is mighty has done great things for me, and holy is his name" (Luke 1:48–49).

According to the context of Luke 1 (especially verses 26–38), "great things" refers to Mary having just conceived Jesus in her womb. Mary's "blessed" state, then, exists solely because of the divine Christ-child within her.

When Mary's cousin Elizabeth encounters Mary soon after Mary conceived Jesus, in Luke 1:42–43, she gives us more insight into just who Mary of Nazareth is when she "exclaim[s] with a loud cry . . . 'Why is this granted me, that the mother of my Lord should come to me?'"

First, we note the reference to Mary as "Mother of the Lord," Jesus Christ. But if we understand its Old Testament antecedent, this God-inspired declaration becomes even more illuminating. Elizabeth was referring, almost verbatim, to a text from 2 Samuel 6:9, wherein David exclaims, concerning the Old Testament Ark of the Covenant, "How can the ark of the LORD come to me?"

The Ark of the Covenant, we know, was especially holy and called *the ark of almighty God* because it contained within it three *types* or prefigurements of Jesus Christ. According to Hebrews 9:4, it contained the high priest Aaron's miraculous staff, a sample of the miraculous bread from heaven—the *manna*—and the Ten Commandments, or "Ten Words" (*dabar* in Hebrew means "word" or "commandment").

Mary carried within her our true High Priest (Heb. 3:1), the true "manna from heaven" (John 6:31–32), and the Word made flesh (John 1:14). Thus, she is the true Ark of the New Covenant.

Mary is correctly called Mother of God because Jesus Christ, her son, is God. To deny this essential truth of the Faith, as the Council of Ephesus (431) declared, is to cut oneself off from full communion with Christ and his Church. In the first of many *anathemas* or condemnations of St. Cyril (the famous fifth-century bishop of Alexandria) that would be accepted by the Council, it decreed:

> If anyone does not confess that God is truly Emmanuel, and that on this account the Holy Virgin is the Mother of God (for according to the flesh

she gave birth to the Word of God become flesh by birth), let him be anathema.

In its definition the council referred to the prophecy of Isaiah 7:14, which prophesied over 700 years before the birth of Christ that the Messiah was to be born of a woman and yet he was to be "God with us." Thus, we have evidence from both the Old and New Testaments testifying to Mary as Mother of God.

The *Catechism of the Catholic Church* (CCC) sums up everything for us:

Called in the Gospels "the mother of Jesus," Mary is acclaimed by Elizabeth, at the prompting of the Spirit and even before the birth of her son, as "the mother of my Lord." In fact, the One whom she conceived as man by the Holy Spirit, who truly became her Son according to the flesh, was none other than the Father's eternal Son, the second person of the Holy Trinity. Hence the Church confesses that Mary is truly "Mother of God" (CCC 495).

2. What is the Immaculate Conception?

The Immaculate Conception refers to Mary's preservation from original sin from the very moment of her conception. The formal definition of this dogma was given to the Church by Pope St. Pius IX in 1854:

We declare, pronounce, and define that the doctrine which holds that the most Blessed Virgin Mary, in the first instance of her conception, by a singular privilege granted by Almighty God, in view of the merits of Jesus Christ, the Savior of the human race, was preserved free from all stain of original sin, is a doctrine revealed by God and therefore to be believed firmly and constantly by all the faithful.[3]

This teaching is very much rooted in Scripture, particularly Luke 1:28–30:

And [the angel Gabriel] came to [Mary] and said, "Hail, full of grace, the Lord is with you!" But she was greatly troubled at the saying, and considered in her mind what sort of greeting this might be. And the angel said to her, "Do not be afraid, Mary, for you have found favor with God."

According to many biblical scholars, what on the surface looks like a simple greeting is much more than that. The angel communicates to Mary a new name or title[4]—in Greek, the greeting was *kaire, kekaritomene*, or "Hail, full of grace." Generally speaking, when one greeted another with *kaire*, a name or title would often be found in the immediate context.[5] The fact that the angel replaces Mary's name in the greeting with "full of grace" is significant.

In Hebrew culture, names and name changes tell us something *permanent* about someone.[6] When you add to this the fact that St. Luke uses the perfect passive participle—*kekaritomene* literally means "she who has been graced" in a completed sense—we have a profound indication of Mary's uniquely holy state.[7] This verbal adjective, "graced," is not just describing a simple past action. Greek has the *aorist* tense for that. The perfect tense is used to indicate that an action has been completed in the past, resulting in a present state of being. That's Mary's name!

So what does it tell us about Mary? Well, the average Christian is *not* completed in grace in a permanent sense (see Phil. 3:8–12). But according to the angel, Mary *is*. You and I sin, not *because* of grace, but because of a *lack* of grace, or a lack of cooperation with grace, in our lives. This greeting of the angel is one clue into the unique character and calling of the Mother of God. Mary was given the *name* "full of grace" and in the perfect tense indicating that this permanent state of Mary was completed.

It is important for us to recall that New Covenant fulfillments are always *more* glorious than—*perfections of,* if you will—their Old Testament types, which are "but a shadow of the good things to come" in the New Covenant (cf. Heb. 10:1). The fall of Adam and Eve is an excellent example of this. In Genesis 3:15 we find, immediately after the fall of our original parents, God telling Satan about the advent of the *antitypes* of Jesus and Mary, or "the woman" (Mary) and her "seed" (Jesus), who would *reverse the curse,* as it is said, that Adam and Eve had brought upon humanity through their disobedience:

> I will put enmity between you and *the woman*, and between your seed and her seed; he shall bruise your head, and you shall bruise his heel.

In the beginning, Adam and Eve are named simply "the man" and "the woman" before the woman's name change to Eve (Heb.—*mother of the living*) after the fall (see Gen. 2:21ff). When we then look at the New Covenant, Jesus is explicitly referred to as the "last Adam," or the "New Adam" in 1 Corinthians 15:45. And Jesus himself indicates Mary to be the prophetic "woman," or "New Eve," of Genesis 3:15, when he refers to his mother as "woman" in John 2:5 and 19:26. Moreover, St. John refers to Mary as "woman" *eight times* in Revelation 12. As the first Eve brought death to all of her children through disobedience and heeding the words of the ancient serpent, the devil, the "New Eve" of Revelation 12 brings life and salvation to all of her children through her obedience.

The same "serpent" who deceived the original woman of Genesis is revealed, in Revelation 12, to fail in his attempt to overcome this *New Woman.* The New Eve overcomes the serpent, and as a result, "The serpent was angry with the woman, and went off to make war on the rest of her offspring, on those who keep the commandments of God, and bear testimony to Jesus" (Rev. 12:17).

Since she is revealed to be the *New Eve*, it would be unthinkable for Mary to be conceived with original sin. If she were, she would be inferior to Eve of old, who was created in a perfect state, free from all sin.

3. How could a mother be a virgin?

Among others we could consider, we will examine three reasons why Mary was and continues to be both a virgin and a mother.

In Luke 1:34, when Mary was told by the angel Gabriel that she was chosen to be the mother of the Messiah, she asked the question, literally translated from the Greek, "How shall this be, since I know not man?" This question makes no sense unless Mary had professed a vow of virginity.

When we consider that Mary and Joseph were already "espoused," according to verse 27 of this same chapter, we understand Mary and Joseph to have had already what would be akin to a ratified marriage. They were married! Normally, in ancient Israel, after the espousal the husband would go off and prepare a home for his new bride, then receive her into his home, where the union would be consummated. Thus we read that Joseph intended to "divorce her quietly" (Matt. 1:19) when he discovered she was pregnant.

This background is significant because a newly married woman would not, when told she would conceive and bear a child, ask the question, "How shall this be?" She would know! Unless, of course, that woman already had a vow of virginity. Mary believed the message but wanted to know how it was going to be accomplished. This indicates she was not planning on the normal course of events for her future with her husband, Joseph.

There are other biblical reasons to believe that Mary and Joseph never consummated their marriage. In John 19:26, from the cross, Jesus gave his mother to the care of St. John even though by law the next eldest siblings, if there were any, would have the responsibility to care for her. It is not an option for Christians to believe that Jesus would take his mother away from his family in disobedience to the law.

Some will claim Jesus did this because his brothers and sisters were not there. They had left him. Thus, Jesus committed his mother to John, who was faithful and present at the foot of the cross.

This claim betrays a very low and unbiblical Christology. As John tells us, Jesus "knew all men" (cf. John 2:25). If St. James were his uterine brother, Jesus would have known he would be faithful along with his "brother" Jude. The fact is, Jesus had no brothers and sisters, so he had the responsibility, on a human level, to take care of his mother. And that he did.

Furthermore, in Luke 1:34, when Mary asked the angel how she was going to conceive a child, the angel responded, "The Holy Spirit will come upon you, and the power of the Most High will overshadow you; therefore the child to be born will be called holy, the Son of God."

The language of "overshadowing" here is nuptial language hearkening back to Ruth 3:9, where Ruth said to Boaz, "spread your skirt over [me]" when she revealed to him his duty to marry her according to the "levirate law" of Deuteronomy 25. Thus Mary is truly and in a unique way the spouse of the Holy Spirit.[8]

Later, when Mary turned up pregnant, Joseph would have been required to divorce her because she would then belong to another (see Deut. 24:1–4; Jer. 3:1). When Joseph found out that "the other" was the Holy Spirit, the idea of Joseph having conjugal relations with Mary would not be a possibility. She belonged to God alone; Joseph would have then been called to be her earthly protector (see 2 Sam. 16:20–22; 18:15; 20:3).

4. What is the Assumption of Mary, and what is the biblical evidence for it?

Mary's Assumption is the dogma that, at the end of her earthly life, God raised Mary to heaven, body and soul. The Bible is quite plain that Mary is in heaven. Revelation 12:1–9:

> And a great sign appeared in heaven, a woman clothed with the sun . . . she was with child . . . And another sign appeared in heaven . . . and the dragon stood before the woman . . . that he might devour her child when she brought it forth; she brought forth a male child [Jesus], one who is to rule all the nations with a rod of iron . . . And the woman fled into the wilderness . . . Now war arose in heaven, Michael and his angels fighting against the dragon . . . And the great dragon was thrown down . . . who is called the Devil and Satan.

There are at least four reasons why Mary is the best fit for the literal identity of "the woman":

1. "The woman" in Revelation 12 "brought forth" Jesus. There can be no doubt Mary was the one who did this.

2. Though we could discover many spiritual levels of meaning for the flight of the woman in 12:6, Mary and the Holy Family *literally* fled into Egypt, with divine assistance, in Matthew 2:13–15.

3. Mary is referred to prophetically as "woman" in Genesis 3:15, Jeremiah 31:22, and by Jesus as the

same in John 2:4 and 19:26. Especially considering the same apostle, St. John, wrote the Gospel of John and the book of Revelation, it is no stretch to say John would have had Mary in mind when he used the familiar term "the woman" for the mother of the "male child."

4. There are four main characters in the chapter: "the woman," the devil, Jesus, and the archangel Michael. No one denies that the other three mentioned are real persons. It fits the context to interpret "the woman" as a person (Mary) as well.

Some will object and claim "the woman" of Revelation 12 is either the Church or, perhaps, ancient Israel. There is truth to both claims, as there are often multiple levels of meaning to biblical texts. Israel is often depicted as the Lord's bride in the Old Testament (cf. Song of Sol., Jer. 3:1, etc.). And Jesus was "brought forth" in Israel. So there is precedent to refer to Israel as "the woman."

The book of Revelation depicts the New Covenant Church as a "woman"—the "bride of Christ" (cf. Rev. 21:2). And "the woman" of Revelation 12 is also depicted as continuing to beget children to this day: all "who keep the commandments of God, and have the testimony of Jesus Christ" (v. 17). The Church certainly fits this description.

But, again, *on the literal level*, Mary is the obvious fit.

But how do we know Mary is *bodily* in heaven? There are lots of souls in heaven, but they don't have their bodies.

Note that "the woman" is depicted as having "the moon under her *feet*, and on her *head* a crown" (v. 1). Elsewhere in Revelation and in other parts of Scripture, saints in heaven are referred to as the "souls of those who had been slain" (Rev. 6:9) or "the spirits of just men made perfect" (Heb. 12:23). And this is to be expected, because until the resurrection they will be disembodied souls or spirits. But "the woman" of Revelation 12 is portrayed as having *a body* with a *head* and *feet*.

But perhaps even more important than this is that, according to Revelation 11:19, the "Ark of the Covenant" is in *heaven*. And this is just one verse prior to the unveiling of "the woman" of Revelation 12:1.

Then God's temple in heaven was opened, and the ark of his covenant was seen within his temple.

In order to appreciate the identity of the Ark, consider the identity of the temple John sees as housing the Ark:

Jesus answered them, "Destroy this temple, and in three days I will raise it up.". . . But he spoke of the temple of his body (John 2:21).

I saw no temple [in heaven], for its temple is the Lord God the Almighty and the lamb (Rev. 21:22).

When John sees the temple in heaven, he is not viewing brick and mortar. He is viewing the true Temple, which is Christ's body. In the same way, he is not seeing the Old Covenant Ark but the new and true Ark of the Covenant. It was Mary's *body*, now in heaven, that housed the Son of God, the fulfillment of the various types of Christ that were contained in the Old Covenant Ark.

5. What does it mean to say that Mary is "Mediatrix"?

The word *mediatrix* is the feminine form of *meditator,* one who serves as a go-between. To some, even just a surface reading of 1 Timothy 2:5 would seem to eliminate the idea of Mary as Mediatrix:

There is one God and one mediator between God and men, the man Jesus Christ.

All Christians agree that Jesus Christ is the sole mediator between God and men *in a strict sense* because Jesus Christ alone unites in himself divinity, which demands reconciliation, and humanity, which needs to be reconciled. However, this in no way means Christ could not empower members of his body, the Church, to participate in his mediation in a subordinate way. As Mediatrix, Mary does this to a preeminent degree.

The context of 1 Timothy 2:5 proves the point. In the first two verses of the chapter, St. Paul commands "supplications, prayers and *intercessions* to be made for all men." *Intercession* is a synonym for *mediation*. Hebrews 7:24–25 refers to Jesus acting as our one mediator at the right hand of the Father and refers to him as *intercessor*:

> But [Christ] holds his priesthood permanently, because he continues for ever. Consequently he is able for all time to save those who draw near to God through him, since he always lives to make intercession for them.

Even though Christ is our one mediator/intercessor, Paul commands *all Christians* to be intercessors/mediators. He goes on to add, in verse 7, "*For this* I was appointed a preacher and apostle." What is an apostle if not a mediator? The very definition of apostle, according to Thayer's *Greek-English Lexicon of the New Testament*, is "a delegate, messenger, one sent forth with orders." That's an essential part of what a mediator is.

Another way of understanding this is to consider that a priest is also, by definition, "a mediator between God and men." And yet, according to 1 Peter 2:5–9, *all Christians are priests.*

[A]nd like living stones be yourselves built into a spiritual house, to be a holy priesthood . . . But you are a chose race, a royal priesthood, a holy nation, God's own people.

Remember, we are not talking about *necessity* here. The Church is not claiming that Christ couldn't get the job done so he needed to enlist the help of his mother and the Body of Christ to mediate graces to other members of Christ. Of course not! He could do it all—and all by himself—if he wanted to. He could come down here right now and write this booklet much more effectively than I ever could. But he *chooses* not to do everything himself, strictly speaking. He delights in using the members of his Body to communicate his life and love to the world.

The idea of members of the Church acting as mediators is ultimately rooted in the radical union the Church has with Christ and each other described by Paul through the analogy of the body:

[God] has put all things under [Christ's] feet and has made him the head over all things for the Church, which is his body, the fullness of him who fills all in all (Eph. 1:22–23).

This radical union with Christ and with the other members of the Body of Christ does not cease at death. Romans 8:35–38 tells us, among other things, "neither death nor life . . . shall be able to separate us from the love of Christ." Thus, those alive on earth can still benefit from—they are still connected to—the other members of the Body of Christ in heaven.

Is Christ, then, our one, true mediator? Absolutely! And it is this same Christ who has chosen to use his Body to mediate God's grace to the world *in and through him*.

So what about Mary? Well, she is certainly a member of the Body of Christ, and so a mediatrix. The difference with her is not a matter of *essence*, but of *degree*. Mary's role is unique because in cooperating with God to bring Christ into the world, she alone among human beings brings the source of all grace to the entire world. Individual Christians are called to mediate grace to various other members of Christ, and to those they encounter who are outside of Christ as well, in accordance with their individual gifts. Mary alone was called to bring *all* grace to the *entire* world. She did not just bring grace to some with whom she came into contact. She brought "grace and truth" (John 1:17) to the world in her son, Jesus Christ.

6. What does it mean to call Mary "co-redemptrix"? Isn't Jesus alone the Redeemer of the world?

By definition, *co-redemptrix* means Mary cooperates with Christ in the salvation of souls. But this does not deny that Jesus alone is the one who redeems and saves the world.

There is no essential difference between calling Mary "co-redemptrix" and St. Paul telling us he and Apollos were co-laborers with Christ (1 Cor. 3:5–9) in the salvation of the Corinthians.[9] *All* Christians are "co-redeemers" with Christ inasmuch as all are called to cooperate with God in bringing souls to him through prayer, obedience, by suffering with Christ, and sharing Christ.[10] Mary alone is given the *title* co-redemptrix because she alone was called to bring Christ to the entire world, as we see in Scripture:

> And behold, you will conceive in your womb and bear a son, and you shall call his name Jesus. . . . And Mary said to the angel, "How can this be. . . ?" And the angel said to [Mary], "The Holy Spirit will come upon you, and the power of the Most High will overshadow you; therefore the child to be born will be called holy, the Son of God. . . . For with God nothing will be impossible." And Mary said, "Behold, I am the handmaid of the Lord; let it be to me according to your word" (Luke 1:31–38).

When Mary said, "[L]et it be done," she opened the way for God to come into the world and save us. This is a textbook definition of Mary acting as *co-redemptrix.*

She cooperated with God's grace in the redemption of the whole world.

This teaching is found in some of the very earliest Christian writings we have. St. Irenaeus of Lyons, writing in A.D. 180, is a great example:

> "Behold the handmaid of the Lord; be it unto me according to thy word." . . . Eve was disobedient . . . as she, having indeed a husband, Adam, but being nevertheless yet a virgin . . . having become disobedient, was made the cause of death, both to herself and to the entire human race. . . . Mary, having a man betrothed [to her], and being nevertheless a virgin, by yielding obedience, became the cause of salvation, both to herself and the whole human race.[11]

Mary's cooperation with the work of her son is also seen at the wedding feast at Cana.

> On the third day there was a marriage at Cana in Galilee, and the mother of Jesus was there. . . . When the wine failed, the mother of Jesus said to him, "They have no wine." And Jesus said to her, "O woman, what have you to do with me? My hour has not yet come." His mother said to the servants, "Do whatever he tells you." . . . Jesus said to them, "Fill the jars with water." . . . When the steward of the feast tasted the water now become wine . . . [he] said

. . . "you have kept the good wine until now." This, the first of his signs, Jesus did at Cana in Galilee, and manifested his glory; and his disciples believed in him (John 2:1–11).

Scripture scholar Fr. William Leonard says the language of the Greek text translated "what have you to do with me" (*ti emoi kai soi gunay*) indicates "a divergence of viewpoints between the two parties concerned." This is a *Hebraism*—a Hebrew phrase transliterated into Greek—used in multiple texts in the Old Testament, always portending a similar meaning (see Judg. 11:12; 2 Sam. 16:10; 19:22; 2 Kings 3:13; 2 Chron. 35:21).

Fr. Leonard further explains that what *seems* to be a refusal on the surface is actually "a refusal *ad mentem*"—a refusal "to a purpose," or "with a purpose in mind."[12]

In short, Jesus here uses the strongest of language to demonstrate Mary's essential role in God's plan of salvation. He simply will not enter into his ministry, perform his first miracle, and bring his disciples to faith, *until Mary intervenes*. "My hour is not yet come," he says. And yet he responds to Mary's intercession and performs his inaugural miracle through her intercession.

Finally, we come to the mystery of the Cross, in which we again find Mary cooperating with Jesus' salvific work.

Simeon blessed them and said to Mary his mother, "Behold, this child is set for the fall and rising of many in Israel, and for a sign that is spoken against (and a sword will pierce through your own soul also), that thoughts out of many hearts may be revealed" (Luke 2:34–35).

The prophet Simeon tells us that "the sign of contradiction," the crucifix, was set to be the sign of salvation for "many" (or "all") in Israel.[13] But in the same breath he reveals that a sword will pierce Mary's soul as well. Why? So that the *thoughts of many hearts would be revealed*.[14] Jesus and Mary would together suffer so that the same "many" would be saved. Once again, we see co-redemptrix in the plainest of terms.

In John 19:27 we find the fulfillment of this prophecy. From the Cross, in that holy hour of immeasurable suffering, Jesus gave Mary to be the spiritual mother of St. John:

"Woman, behold, your son!" Then he said to the disciple, "Behold, your mother!"

But according to Revelation 12:17, there's more. Here we see that John represents not just himself, but all Christians. The same apostle would write:

Then the dragon was angry with the woman, and

went off to make war on the rest of her offspring, *on those who keep the commandments of God and bear testimony to Jesus.*

Mary, co-redemptrix, "gives birth" to all Christians in fulfillment of Simeon's prophecy.

7. Is there a queen in the kingdom of heaven?

If Jesus is the king of heaven and earth, then we know who Mary is: the *queen mother*. It really is that simple. Pope Pius XII pithily summarized why Christians ought to honor Mary as queen:

According to ancient tradition and the sacred liturgy the main principle on which the royal dignity of Mary rests is without doubt her divine motherhood. In holy writ, concerning the son whom Mary will conceive, we read this sentence: "He shall be called the son of the most high, and the Lord God shall give unto him the throne of David his father, and he shall reign in the house of Jacob forever, and of his kingdom there will be no end," and in addition Mary is called "Mother of the Lord," from this it is easily concluded that she is a queen, since she bore a son who, at the very moment of his conception, because of the hypostatic union of the human nature with the Word, was also as man, king and lord of all things . . . it can be said that the heavenly voice of the Archangel Gabriel was the first to proclaim Mary's royal office.[15]

Revelation 12 further demonstrates Mary's queenship:

And a great sign appeared in heaven, a woman clothed with the sun, with the moon under her feet, and on her head a crown of twelve stars; she was with child. . . . [S]he brought forth a male child, one who is to rule all the nations with a rod of iron, but her child was caught up to God and to his throne. . . . Then the dragon was angry with the woman, and went off to make war on the rest of her offspring, on those who keep the commandments of God and bear testimony to Jesus (Rev. 12:1–2; 5:17).

Here Mary is clearly depicted as a cosmic queen giving birth to both Christ and all Christians, all the while wearing her regal crown. She rules and reigns with her divine son at the center of the perennial battle between the kingdom of God and the kingdoms of this world in union with the serpent of old.

It can be difficult for us in the modern Western world to understand ancient monarchical concepts. But first-century Jews knew that a kingdom meant that there would be both a king and a *queen mother*. It was an integral part of their history as God's people.

Now when Athaliah the mother of Ahaziah saw that her son was dead, she arose and destroyed all the royal family. But Jehosheba, the daughter of King Joram, sister of Ahaziah, took Joash the son of Ahaziah, and stole him away from among the king's sons who were about to be slain. . . . Thus she hid him from Athaliah, so that he was not slain; and he remained with her six years, hid in the house of the Lord, while Athaliah reigned over the land (2 Kings 11:1–4).

Queen Athaliah ruled in Israel for six years after her son King Ahaziah died. She was a wicked woman and so may not seem to be the greatest type of the Blessed Mother. But then there were many wicked kings in ancient Israel, too, who were nonetheless types of Christ. (Even the great King David himself is quite well known for his moral failings.) Leaving aside Athaliah's wickedness, we see in this text a scriptural example of the importance and the authority of the queen mother.[16]

Perhaps the most profound example of the power of the queen mother in the Old Testament can be found personified in Bathsheba, the wife of David and queen mother to Solomon. In 1 Kings 1, when Bathsheba desired a favor of King David, she needed to enlist the help of Nathan the prophet:

Bathsheba bowed and did obeisance to the king, and the king said, "What do you desire?" . . . While she was still speaking with the king, Nathan the prophet came in (1 Kings 1:16-22).

After David died, however, we saw a dramatically different story:

So Bathsheba went to King Solomon, to speak to him on behalf of Adonijah. And the king rose to meet her, and bowed down to her; then he sat on his throne and had a seat brought for the king's mother; and she sat on his right. Then she said, "I have one small request to make of you; do not refuse me." And the king said to her, "Make your request, my mother; for I will not refuse you" (1 Kings 2:13–23).

As one of many wives of the king, Bathsheba was a beggar. As queen mother, she enjoyed the king's honor and obedience. This is a beautiful image of the office not only of the Old Covenant queen, but of the New Covenant queen mother, Mary.

8. How can God have a mother?

We often hear this objection to calling Mary the Mother of God: "A dog gives birth to a dog, a cat to a cat, a human to a human. So Mary would have to *be* God in order to give birth to God!" How do we respond?

This question always brings to mind a debate I watched back in the '80s on the *John Ankerberg Show,* a Protestant apologetics television broadcast, between Walter Martin and Fr. Mitch Pacwa. Still a Protestant at the time, I was rooting for Martin—then one of the leading Evangelical apologists in the world and a mentor of mine.

During the debate Martin claimed that Mary was the mother of Jesus' *human nature* only, and so could not be called Mother of God. As part of his argument he presented the classic syllogism used by the Church for well over a millennium and a half:

Major premise: Jesus is God
Minor premise: Mary is the mother of Jesus
Conclusion: Mary is the mother of God

But then he presented another syllogism that in his mind followed necessarily from the first, and one that if held would prove devastating to New Testament theology:

Major premise: God is Trinity
Minor premise: Mary is the mother of God
Conclusion: Mary is the mother of the Trinity

I can remember thinking, as I watched the debate, "Yeah, Pacwa, explain that one away!"

In his response, Fr. Pacwa explained that Mary is only the mother of the *second person* of the Blessed Trinity incarnate, because the Father and the Holy Spirit did not become incarnate. In his syllogism, Martin did not properly distinguish the term "God" in his major and minor premises. The term "God" in the major premise refers to all three persons of the Blessed Trinity, whereas in the minor premise "God" is used within the title "Mother of God." In that context, "God" refers *only* to the second person of the Blessed Trinity, who *is* God but who *isn't* the Trinity.

When we say *God*, we may be referring to all three persons of the Blessed Trinity, but not necessarily so. The three persons in the Trinity are distinct within the eternal relations, so we can speak of them individually. Thus, we can say Mary is the mother of only the *second person* of the Trinity. But we must also remember that the three persons share the same divine nature; hence, they are each fully God. There are not three Gods, nor are there "parts" with God. He is absolutely one in essence or nature. Thus, we can call Mary *Mother of God* without making her the mother of the Trinity.

This point of confusion is relatively simple to clear up, but Protestants might still perceive an apparent weakness in the argument, as Walter Martin did during the debate. Even if Mary is the mother of only the second person of the Blessed Trinity, that person is just as eternal as the other two divine persons. Mary, objected Martin, would still have to be eternal in order to be his mother. Thus, we really haven't answered the objection that in order to give birth to God, Mary would have to *be* God.

Yet the Catholic Church does not say Mary is the source of the divine nature (which is eternal) of the second person of the Blessed Trinity. That would be both heretical and absurd. But it does not then follow that she cannot be his mother.

We can use the example of normal human reproduction to help clarify this point. When a woman bears a child, she is not the source of the child's immortal soul. God, the source of all life, directly creates each individual soul.[17] However, we do not conclude from this that the mother is merely the mother of the *body* of the child. Instead she is the mother of a whole *person* who is a body-soul composite.

Analogously, though Mary did not provide Jesus with either his divine nature or his immortal human soul, she was more than the mother of a body. Mary, like any other mother, gave birth to a person; and that person is God.

And this leads to the real crux of the issue. Ultimately, rejecting Mary as Mother of God results in one of three serious Christological errors:

1. The denial of the divinity of Christ

2. The creation of two persons to represent Jesus Christ, one human and one divine

3. Some form of unintelligible Christology leaving Jesus Christ as something less than a fully divine person

Understanding Mary to be Mother of God guards and defends the truth that Jesus Christ is the second person of the Blessed Trinity incarnate. That person must be understood to be God—or else you've got the wrong person.

9. How can Mary be without sin?

In Romans 3:23, St. Paul famously declared, "All have sinned and fall short of the glory of God." 1 John 1:8 says, "If we say we have no sin, we deceive ourselves, and the truth is not in us," and Romans 3:10 adds, "None is righteous, no not one."

In light of these Scripture verses, our Protestant friends will say, Mary couldn't have been sinless as Catholics believe she was. She must have been a sinner like every other human being, and needed redemption.

How should Catholics respond to these prooftexts?

When I'm asked about Romans 3:23, I like to respond with the same series of questions that a young Catholic Marine named Sgt. Matt Dula asked me nearly thirty years ago, when I was serving in the United

States Marine Corps and just starting on my road to Rome. The conversation went something like this:

Matt: "Do you mean to tell me that you believe Jesus Christ was a sinner? I've never heard of a Christian believing that before."

Tim: "Of course not!"

Matt: "Well, if you believe literally that 'if any man says he has no sin, he is a liar' . . . I have to ask you: was Jesus Christ fully man?"

Tim: "Well, yes, but he was also *God*."

Matt: "Yes, and Mary is the *Mother of God*, but that is not the question. Was Jesus *fully man*? If he was, and we are going to take 1 John 1:8 in a strict, literal sense, then Jesus was a sinner."

Tim: "Okay, I see your point, but Jesus was an *exception* to Romans 3:10, 3:23, and 1 John 1:8. The Bible tells us so in Hebrews 4:15, which clearly says Christ was 'tempted as we are, yet without sinning.'"

Matt: "Oh, so you admit there are exceptions, do you? What if I were to show you that there are *millions* of exceptions to these verses?"

Matt then explained to me what I have explained to thousands since. First of all, we need to know that all three of those prooftexts are dealing with personal sin, not original sin. (Romans 5:12 deals with original sin, and we can demonstrate exceptions there as well.) 1 John 1:8 clearly refers to personal sin because in the very next verse John tells us, "If we confess our sins, he is faithful and just to forgive us our sins." We don't *confess* original sin because we didn't do it! Confession is only for personal sins.

The context of Romans 3:23, that it refers to personal sin, can be seen a few verses prior:

> None is righteous, no, not one; no one understands, no one seeks for God. All have turned aside, together they have gone wrong; no one does good, not even one. Their throat is an open grave. They use their tongues to deceive. The venom of asps is under their lips. Their mouth is full of curses and bitterness (Rom. 3:10–14).

Original sin is not something we *do*; it is something we've inherited. As a result of the sin of Adam, we possess a fallen nature. That is the essence of original sin.[18]

After explaining all of this, Matt asked, "Has a baby in the womb, or a child of two, ever committed a personal sin?"

"No, they have not," I had to concede.[19]

"Or how about the severely mentally challenged who do not have the use of their intellects and wills; have they committed personal sins?"

Once again, I had to agree the answer was no. In order to commit a sin, a person must have knowledge of the sinful act and full use of his will in performing that objectively sinful act.

"There!" declared Matt. "Millions of exceptions to Romans 3:23 and 1 John 1:8!"[20]

My response at this point was similar to the response I often get today: "Well, that may be, but you can't show me why *Mary* is another exception." I didn't realize it at the time (it would hit me later like a ton of bricks), but in so saying, my three "go-to" texts against Mary Immaculate went up in smoke!

10. If Jesus had "brothers," wouldn't that mean that Mary had other children?

Protestant apologist Eric Svendsen plainly states: "The New Testament mentions several times that Jesus had biological brothers and sisters."[21] Matthew 13:55–56 says:

> "Is not this the carpenter's son? Is not his mother called Mary? And are not his brethren James and Joseph and Simon and Judas? And are not all his sisters with us?"

On the surface, these texts seem troubling for the Catholic position. If Jesus had brothers, how could Mary have remained a virgin?

We must first remember that the Gospels weren't originally written in English but Greek, and that the common language of Christ and his contemporaries was Aramaic. And in both Aramaic and the Greek of the New Testament, the word used for *brother* was also commonly used to mean cousins, uncles, nephews, and other relatives. This probably stemmed, at least in part, from the fact that neither Aramaic nor Hebrew had a specific word for *cousin*. It became common to use *brother* or *sister* when speaking of cousins, which led to using the term for other family relations as well.[22] The *Catechism* cites Abraham and Lot as classic examples of this, in Genesis 13:8 and 14:16. Though they were uncle and nephew by relation, they called one another *brother* (CCC 500).

It is not a surprise, then, that in both the Septuagint (the Greek translation of the Hebrew scriptures) and in the New Testament, even though there was a word for "cousin" in Greek (*anepsios*, as found in Colossians 4:10), we find the same phenomenon. In the Septuagint, we have multiple examples. Leviticus 10:4 uses a form of *adelphos* ("brother") to refer to the cousins of Moses and Aaron. In 1 Chronicles 23:22, the cousins of the daughters of Eleazar are called *adelphoi*. And in Tobit 7:2–4 we have forms of both *anepsios* and *adelphos* used as synonyms within two verses of each other: "Then Raguel said to his wife Edna, 'How much the young man resembles my *cousin* Tobit!' . . . So he said to them, 'Do you know our *brother* Tobit?'"

The New Testament also clearly uses *adelphos* to refer generally to *relatives*, just as the Septuagint does. For example, John 19:25 refers to "[Jesus'] mother's sister (*adelphe*), Mary the wife of Clopas," being present at the foot of the cross along with Mary and Mary Magdalene. It is highly unlikely that there would be two *uterine* sisters with the same name of *Mary.* This is surely an example of some other kind of relation being called *sister.*[23]

Further, after Matthew 13:55 mentions the brothers of the Lord, "James and Joseph and Simon and Judas," verse 27:56 tells us who their mother was: "Mary, the mother of James and Joseph"—*not* the mother of Jesus, or mother of the Lord. Yet the children of this other Mary are called *brothers of the Lord.* Thus, the go-to text so often used by Protestants to "prove" Mary had other children is actually just another example of *brother* being used as *relative* or *cousin* in the Greek New Testament.

Galatians 1:17–19 is another biblical prooftext often used to argue that Jesus had at least one uterine brother:[24]

Nor did I go up to Jerusalem to those who were apostles before me, but I went away into Arabia;

and again I returned to Damascus. Then after three years I went up to Jerusalem to visit Cephas, and remained with him fifteen days. But I saw none of the other apostles except James the Lord's brother.

But notice that James, whom Paul calls a *brother of the Lord*, is an *apostle*.

Now, there were some called apostles, such as Barnabas, who were not of the twelve.[25] But here Paul is writing about an experience he had shortly after his conversion when he speaks of *not* going to Jerusalem to those who "were apostles before [him]." This would have been, at most, only one to three years after the Resurrection of Christ.[26] The apostles were still in Jerusalem at that time.[27] It is unlikely, then, that Paul is referring here to later "apostles" in an extended sense.[28] He is referring to James, the *Lord's brother*, as being one of the twelve apostles.[29]

From there it's a matter of simple deduction. There were only two apostles named James among the twelve. The first was the son of Zebedee. But he could not be the James Paul speaks about in Galatians 1, because according to Acts 12:1–2 he was martyred very early. That leaves the other apostle James. And according to Luke 6:15–16, his father's name was Alphaeus—not Joseph. That means that the apostle James whom Paul calls *the Lord's brother* could not have been Jesus' uterine brother.[30]

11. What other arguments do Protestants make against the perpetual virginity of Mary?

We read in Matthew 1:18:

> Before they came together [Mary] was found to be
> with child of the Holy Spirit.

Eric Svendsen claims that "before they came to-gether" makes sense only "if Mary *did not* make a vow of lifelong virginity. Matthew is making a point of letting his readers know that the child was conceived before any sexual union took place."[31]

Svendsen might have a point if the word *before* necessarily implied that circumstances changed *after*. But just as in English, the Greek word for *before* (*prin*) does not necessitate any event *after* the time of emphasis. It can be used to emphasize either a present or past event or a state of being rather than a future event.

For example, consider this statement: "Tom dropped out of high school before he graduated." This statement uses the word *before* to emphasize what Tom did in a particular time in his life. In no way does it imply that he *later* graduated from a different school, got his GED, or anything else.

Svendsen is half-right: Matthew's purpose is to emphasize the virginal conception of Jesus. But there is no evidence that the text is concerned with whether or not Joseph and Mary had a sexual union at a later time. There would need to be more information to demonstrate whether or not that took place.

A similar and equally common argument involves the word *until*, as it appears in Matthew 1:24–25:

> When Joseph woke from sleep, he did as the angel of the Lord commanded him; he took his wife, but knew her not until she had borne a son; and he called his name Jesus.

The late Christian apologist Dave Hunt made a lot of hay from these verses, claiming that they meant "Mary was a virgin until the time that Jesus was born. Subsequently, she had a number of other children by Joseph, her husband."[32]

Does Matthew's use of the word *until* mean that Joseph eventually did come to know Mary conjugally? No; as with the word *before,* this implication is unfounded. The word *until* can be used to mean "leading up to the time of" without implying a change afterward. For example, I may say to a friend, "Until we meet again, God bless you!" Does that mean that after we meet again, I want God to *stop* blessing him?

The fourth-century Father of the Church and great Scripture scholar St. Jerome responded to this very question:

And the savior in the Gospel tells the apostles, "Lo, I am with you always, even unto the end of the world." Will the Lord then after the end of the world has come forsake his disciples, and at the very time when seated on twelve thrones they are to judge the twelve tribes of Israel will they be bereft of the company of their Lord?

I could give countless instances of this usage . . . a cloud of proofs; I shall, however, add only a few, and leave the reader to discover others for himself.[33]

Here are some of the plain biblical examples confirming St. Jerome's words:

2 Samuel 6:23: "And Michal the daughter of Saul had no child to the day of her death." Does this mean she had children after she died?

1 Timothy 4:13: "Till I come, attend to the public reading of Scripture, to preaching, to teaching." Does this mean Timothy should stop teaching after St. Paul arrives?

1 Corinthians 15:25: "For he [Christ] must reign until he has put all his enemies under his feet." Does this mean Christ's reign will end after that happens?

Matthew 28:20: "And lo, I am with you always, to the end of the age." As St. Jerome asked, does this verse mean Christ will not be with us after the end of the age?

1 Timothy 6:14: "I charge you to keep the commandments unstained and free from reproach until the appearing of our Lord Jesus Christ." Does this mean they can break the commandments after Jesus comes?

12. Doesn't the Bible condemn the idea that Mary was assumed into heaven?

For many Christians, the doctrine of the Assumption of Mary is more than merely wrong-headed; it is downright blasphemous. And there are two texts of Scripture they commonly use to argue the point:

> No one has ascended up to heaven, but he who descended from heaven, the Son of Man (1 John 3:13).

If "no man" has ascended into heaven, wouldn't that include Mary?

> For as in Adam all die, so also in Christ shall all be made alive. But each in his own order: Christ the first fruits; then at his coming those who belong to Christ (1 Cor. 15:22–23).

If no one except Christ will be resurrected bodily before the Second Coming of Christ, would that not eliminate the possibility of Mary's having been bodily assumed into heaven?

As for John 3:13, this verse does not eliminate the possibility of the Assumption of Mary, for four reasons.

1. John was quoting the actual words our Lord spoke when he wrote, "No one has ascended into heaven, but . . . the Son of man." Jesus was merely saying that no one had ascended into heaven by the time he made that statement. That was long before the Assumption of Mary.

2. Jesus cannot be saying that no one else will *ever* be taken to heaven. If that is the case, then what is all this Christianity stuff about, anyway?

3. It would be acceptable to interpret John 3:13 as referring to Christ's unique Ascension. We would then have to ask the question: what is it about Jesus' Ascension that is unique? Well, the fact that he *ascended* is unique. Mary did not *ascend* to heaven. She was *assumed*. There is a big difference. Jesus ascended by his own divine power, as he prophesied he would in John 2:19–21: "Destroy this temple, and in three days I will raise it up . . . he spoke of the temple of his body." Mary was powerless to raise herself to heaven; she had to be *assumed*. The same could be said of all Christians. Jesus raised

himself from the dead. Christians will be entirely passive when it comes to their collective resurrection.

4. Here John is demonstrating the divinity of Christ. Historically, we know that he was writing against his archenemy, the heretic Cerinthus, who denied the divinity of Christ. John quotes these words from Jesus to demonstrate that he "descended" from heaven and was both in heaven and on Earth as the "only begotten Son" (cf. 3:16) sharing his Father's nature (cf. 5:17–18). Thus, he was truly God. John also emphasizes that even while "the Son of Man" walked the Earth with his disciples in Galilee, he possessed the beatific vision in his human nature. In that sense, his human nature (Son of Man) had already "ascended" into heaven inasmuch as it possessed the beatific vision, which is at the core of what heaven is. That is John's theme in the text, not whether someone years after Christ could be assumed into heaven or not.

To the argument based on 1 Corinthians 15:22–23 we can respond with at least three points:

1. We must remember that in Scripture there are sometimes exceptions to general theological norms. For example, consider Matthew 3:5–6: "Then went out to [St. John the Baptist] Jerusalem and all Judea

and all the region about the Jordan, and they were baptized by him." We know that "all" here does not mean "every single person" in a strict sense because we know, at least, that Herod, Herodias, and her daughter were exceptions to this verse (see Matt. 14:1–11). They had conspired to put John the Baptist to death! Moreover, in Luke 7:30 many of the Pharisees and Sadducees are explicitly said not to have been baptized by him.

So Mary could be (and is, as we will see below) an exception to 1 Corinthians 15:22–23.

2. We have examples of other "assumptions" in Scripture. Both Enoch (cf. Gen. 5:24) and Elijah were taken up "into heaven" (2 Kings 2:11) in a manner quite out of the ordinary. And so are the "two witnesses" of Revelation 11:3–13. Why couldn't God do this with Mary?

3. We know that Mary is an exception to the "norm" of 1 Corinthians 15:22–23 because in Revelation 12 she is depicted as having been assumed into heaven: "And a great portent appeared in heaven, a woman clothed with the sun . . . she was with child . . . and . . . brought forth a male child [Jesus], one who is to rule all the nations with a rod of iron" (12:1–5). Who was the woman who gave birth to Jesus? Mary! And there she is in heaven!

13. Doesn't the Bible condemn the idea of a "Queen of Heaven"?

Earlier we saw multiple reasons why Catholics honor Mary with the title *Queen of Heaven and Earth*. This dignity gifted to Mary by God is deeply biblical and has been understood in the Church for 2,000 years, but many Protestants I speak to cannot get past one biblical text from the Old Testament that casts a shadow over this topic. And that text is Jeremiah 7:18:

> Do you not see what they are doing in the streets of Judah and in the streets of Jerusalem? The children gather wood, the fathers kindle fire, and the women knead dough, to make cakes for the queen of heaven; and they pour out drink offerings to other gods, to provoke me to anger.

In *Roman Catholics and Evangelicals—Agreements and Differences*, Norman Geisler and Ralph MacKenzie claim, "To call Mary 'Queen of Heaven,' knowing that this very phrase comes from an old pagan idolatrous cult condemned in the Bible (cf. Jer. 7:18), only invites the charge of Mariolatry. And Mariolatry is idolatry."[34]

I can certainly sympathize with their thinking here. I once thought the same. But the truth is: this text has absolutely nothing to do with the Blessed Mother as Queen of Heaven, for at least three reasons:

1. Jeremiah here condemns the adoration of the Mesopotamian goddess Astarte.[35] She is in no way related to Mary. In fact, "she" did not and does not exist in reality. Mary, on the other hand, was a real historical person who was—and is—a queen by virtue of the fact that her son was—and is—the king, as we have seen.

2. Jeremiah condemned *offering sacrifice* to "the queen of heaven." In Scripture, we have many examples of the proper way we should honor great members of the kingdom of God. We give "double honor" to "elders who rule well" in the Church (1 Tim. 5:17). St. Paul tells us we should "esteem very highly" those who are "over [us] in the Lord" (1 Thess. 5:12–13). We sing praises to great members of the family of God who have gone before us (Psalm 45:17). We bow down to them with reverence (1 Kings 2:19). We carry out the work of the Lord in their names (Matt. 10:40–42, DRV), and more. But there is one thing we ought never to do: *offer sacrifice* to them. Offering sacrifice is tantamount to the adoration that is due God alone. And this is precisely what Jeremiah was condemning. The Catholic Church does not

teach—*and has never taught*—that we give Mary the adoration due to God, or that we should offer sacrifice to her.[36]

3. To Geisler and MacKenzie, and to millions of Evangelicals and Fundamentalists, the mere fact that worshipping someone called "queen of heaven" is condemned in Jeremiah 7 eliminates the *possibility* of Mary being the true Queen of Heaven and Earth. This simply does not follow. The existence of a counterfeit queen does not mean there can't be an authentic one. This reasoning followed to its logical end would lead to abandoning the entire Christian Faith! We could not have a Bible because Hinduism, Islam, and many other false religions have "holy books." We could not call Jesus *Son of God* because Zeus and Hera had Apollo, Isis and Osiris had Horus, etc. The fact that there was a false "queen of heaven" worshipped in ancient Mesopotamia does not negate the reality of the true queen who is honored as such in the kingdom of God.

As we noted in an earlier answer, the Catholic Church teaches that Mary is Queen of Heaven and Earth because Scripture reveals her to be the mother of Jesus Christ, who is clearly revealed to be "the King of kings and Lord of lords" (Rev. 19:16). The king, Jesus, established a *kingdom* according to the New

Testament, thereby, gifting his mother with a unique office: Queen Mother.[37]

14. How can Mary hear and answer our prayers in heaven?

Most Protestants presume that prayer should be directed only to God and never to the saints or to Mary. Eric Svendsen objects to the notion of praying to Mary, furthermore, by claiming that she couldn't hear all the prayers directed at her without being God:

> Suppose someone in the United States were to pray to Mary at a certain time during the day. Suppose further that, at exactly that same moment, someone in Europe begins also to pray to Mary . . . suppose at that same moment hundreds of thousands of devoted Catholics all over the world begin praying the rosary. . . . In order for Mary to hear all those prayers at once she would have to be omniscient ("all-knowing")— an attribute that is the property of God alone.[38]

The simplest Catholic response would be to first reference Revelation 5:8:

> And when [Christ, the Lamb] had taken the scroll, the four living creatures and the twenty-four elders fell down before the Lamb, each holding a harp,

and with golden bowls full of incense, which are the prayers of the saints.

I should note here the obvious: the image of these "elders" possessing "golden bowls of incense" representing "the prayers of the saints" is metaphorical. In order for these pure spirits in heaven to offer these "prayers of the saints" to God, they must be intellectually comprehended and then communicated.

These twenty-four elders are clearly human beings in heaven, and they are depicted as "each holding a harp" and "incense, *which are the prayers of the saints*." Thus, each one of them is hearing and responding to multiple prayers from multiple people *at the same time*. What does that mean? It means these saints in heaven—Mary included, of course—somehow have the power to do what Eric Svendsen claims to be "the property of God alone."

And when you think about it, why wouldn't Mary and the saints in heaven be doing just this? If Jesus is in heaven at the right hand of God and "he always lives to make intercession for [us]," as Hebrews 7:25 says, would not Mary and the saints want to do what Jesus does? 1 John 3:1–2 tells us the saints in heaven "will be like him, for [they] shall see him as he is." The real question in my mind is: why would the saints in heaven see Jesus interceding for God's people on earth and just sit around and watch him without joining in on the prayer?

But we still haven't answered Svendsen's main objection. We need to demonstrate the reasonableness of Revelation 5:8. If divine omniscience were required to be able to hear multiple prayers simultaneously, it is true, only God would be up to the task. Even more, God could not communicate this power outside of the godhead because that would be tantamount to creating another infinite God, which is absurd. God alone is the one, true, and infinite God by nature, and there can be no other (cf. Isa. 45:22).

So what gives?

First of all, even one billion is a *finite number*. So it would not require *infinite* power to be able to hear the prayers of a billion people at the same time. That seems simple enough.

To his credit, Eric Svendsen responded to this very argument, made by Catholic apologist Patrick Madrid, in a very insightful way:

> But Madrid's suggestion creates so many consequent theological difficulties that it is difficult to believe he could be satisfied with it. One may as well argue that omniscience is not needed even by God himself since all things that can be known—no matter how many—are nevertheless limited to a finite number.
>
> In spite of Madrid's assertions to the contrary, one must indeed be omniscient or omnipresent (or both) before he can hear more than one prayer at a time.[39]

53

St. Thomas Aquinas answers this question succinctly when he says the ability to perform actions that transcend nature comes from a finite "created light of glory received into [the] created intellect."[40] It would require infinite power to "create the light" or the grace given to empower men and angels to act beyond their given natures. Only God can do that. But it does not require infinite power to passively receive that light. As long as what is received is not infinite by nature or does not require infinite power to comprehend or act upon, it would not be beyond the ability of men (or angels) to receive.

Therefore, we can conclude that this "created light" given by God to empower men and angels to be able to hear millions of prayers and respond to them is reasonable as well as biblical.

15. Isn't it blasphemous to say Mary "redeems" or "saves" us?

Fact is, *all Christians,* not just Mary, are called to "save" souls in cooperation with the grace of Christ. But if you don't understand God's plan of salvation, you will never understand Mary's role in that plan.

There are seven essential points to understanding God's salvific plan.

1. The sufficiency of Christ's sacrifice

Catholics and most Protestants generally agree on this point. Christ's sacrifice is infinitely efficacious for the forgiveness of sins.

1 John 2:1–2 tells us Christ's sacrifice is "the propitiation for our sins, and not only our sins, but the sins of the whole world."

2. God's universal salvific will

Scripture is clear that God both positively "wills all to be saved and come to the knowledge of the truth" (1 Tim. 2:4) and negatively is "not willing that any perish, but that all should come to repentance" (2 Pet. 3:9).

3. Free will

From God's commandment to Adam in Genesis 2:17 not to eat "of the tree of the knowledge of good and evil" lest he die, to God's word to Israel in Deuteronomy 30:19 to choose between life and death, to our Lord telling us in Revelation 3:20, "Behold, I stand at the door and knock; if any one hears my voice and opens the door, I will come in to him," the Bible is clear: man is free either to accept or reject God's call to follow him.

Our Lord himself removed all doubt concerning man's freedom when he revealed that as God from all eternity he willed to gather "Jerusalem" as his own, but they refused him:

Jerusalem, Jerusalem, killing the prophets and stoning those who are sent to you! How often I would have gathered your children together as a hen gathers her brood under her wings, and you would not! (Matt. 23:37).

4. The necessity of human cooperation

Justification, or salvation, is the work of God first and foremost, but it's also the work of man exercising his free will, aided by grace, in an ongoing cooperation with God's initiative:[41] "Work out your own salvation with fear and trembling; for God is at work in you, both to will and to work for his good pleasure" (Phil. 2:12).[42]

- "Since we have these promises, beloved, let us cleanse ourselves from every defilement of body and spirit, and make holiness perfect in the fear of God" (2 Cor. 7:1–2).

- "Having purified your souls by your obedience to the truth . . . love one another earnestly from the heart" (1 Pet. 1:22).

- "Take heed to yourself and to your teaching; hold to that, for by so doing you will save both yourself and your hearers" (1 Tim. 4:16).[43]

Notice, these texts do not say, "God has cleansed

you . . . purified you . . . saved you," though it would be entirely true to say just that. But instead we find Christians "cleanse," "purify," and "save" *themselves*, precisely because they are integrally, freely, and causally involved in the process.

5. How works work

It is no secret that Martin Luther eliminated all works as having anything to do with our justification/salvation. Commenting on St. Paul's Letter to the Romans, Luther wrote:

> The assertion that justification is free to all that are justified leaves none to work, merit or prepare themselves. . . . For if we are justified without works, all works are condemned, whether small or great; Paul exempts none, but thunders impartially against all.[44]

Paul's point in saying that justification is a free gift was not to eliminate works, or man's free cooperation, as necessary for salvation *in all categories*. Men must, for example, choose to open the free gift (see Rev. 3:20; 2 Cor. 6:1; etc.). Paul was answering "Judaizers"—believers in Christ who were attempting to re-establish the law of the Old Covenant as necessary for salvation in the New.[45] Although Paul did make clear that any works done either *before* entering into Christ or *apart* from

57

Christ profit nothing for salvation, works accomplished *in Christ* represent an entirely different category.[46]

> For he will render to every man according to his works: to those who by patience in well-doing seek for glory and honor and immortality, he will give eternal life (Rom. 2:6–7).

6. Merit

When the Catholic Church speaks of "merit," it means nothing more than the reward God guarantees to those who, while first in a state of grace, cooperate with grace via a faith formed by charity.[47]

> Do not be deceived; God is not mocked, for whatever a man sows, that he will also reap. For he who sows to his own flesh will from the flesh reap corruption; but he who sows to the Spirit will from the Spirit reap eternal life. And let us not grow weary in well-doing, for in due season we shall reap, if we do not lose heart (Rom. 6:7–9).[48]

7. Christians save souls through Christ

Once we understand the biblical truth that all Christians really can and must merit eternal reward in and through Christ, we can then understand the many biblical examples of how Christians, including Mary, can merit the grace of salvation for others.[49]

- "And convince some, who doubt; save some, by snatching them out of the fire" (Jude 22–23).

- "I have become all things to all men that I might by all means save some" (1 Cor. 9:22).

- "Take heed to yourself and to your teaching: hold to that, for by so doing you will save both yourself and your hearers" (1 Tim. 4:16).[50]

16. What did the Fathers of the Church say about Mary?

The Fathers of the Church—leaders, teachers, and writers during Christianity's first few centuries after the apostles—were effusive in their support for the Catholic understanding of Mary that has come to us many centuries later.

Mary, Mother of God
St. Ignatius of Antioch (ca. A.D. 107):

> For *our God*, Jesus Christ, was, according to the appointment of God, conceived in the womb by Mary, of the seed of David, but by the Holy Ghost. He *was born* and baptized, that by his passion he might purify the water.[51]

"God . . . was born." You do the math.

St. Irenaeus, bishop of Lyons (A.D. 177):

> The Virgin Mary . . . being obedient to his word, received from an angel the glad tidings that she was to bear God.[52]

Sub Tuum (A.D. 250)
This ancient Coptic Catholic prayer was sung as a hymn:

> Under your mercy, we take refuge, Mother of God, do not reject our supplications in necessity. But deliver us from danger, [O you] alone pure and alone blessed.[53]

The Immaculate Conception
If we consider just Mary's ancient title of *New Eve* taught by the Fathers from both East and West, the Fathers are unanimous.

Not all explicitly conclude Mary to be sinless from the image of "the New Eve," but it follows nonetheless. If you understand that all Old Testament "types" are inferior to their New Testament fulfillments, to say Mary would have been conceived in sin and to have fallen into sin would make her inferior to Eve, who did not receive nearly the grace that Mary received.

Here are two of the earliest examples:

The Epistle of Mathetes to Diognetus (A.D. 140):

> Whereof if thou bear the tree and pluck the fruit, thou shalt ever gather the harvest which God looks for, which [the] serpent toucheth not, nor deceit infecteth, *neither is Eve corrupted, but is believed on as a virgin*, and salvation is set forth.[54]

This ancient text does not explicitly name the New Eve as Mary, but she is implied in the reference to her being "believed on as a virgin." She is depicted as being the opposite of Eve, who had been corrupted.

St. Ephrem of Syria (ca. 360):

> Mary and Eve, two people without guilt, two simple people, were identical. Later, however, one became the cause of our death, the other the cause of our life.[55]

The Perpetual Virginity
On this point, the Fathers of the Church were also *unanimous*. Here are three early examples:

The Protoevangelium of James (ca. A.D. 140)
According to the renowned Patristics scholar Johannes Quasten, "The principal aim of the whole writing is to prove the perpetual and inviolate virginity of Mary before, in, and after the birth of Christ."[56]

St. Clement of Alexandria (A.D. 200)

Clement presents Mary as a sort of archetype of the scriptures, which also *give birth* (to the truth) yet *remain virginal*. He similarly viewed Mary as the archetype of the Church, the ever-virginal bride of Christ. Both were virgins who give birth yet remain virgins: "She (the Church) is virgin and Mother simultaneously; a virgin undefiled and a mother full of love."[57]

Origen (ca. 230):

> Mary, as those declare who with sound mind extol her, had no other son but Jesus.[58]

The Assumption

Recently discovered Syriac fragments of written stories about the Assumption of Mary have now been dated as early as the *third century.*[59] Far from rejecting the Assumption, we find the opposite among the Fathers.

Timothy of Jerusalem (ca. 350–390)

We now have what some believe to be a fourth-century homily on the prophet Simeon and the Blessed Virgin Mary by this priest of Jerusalem, which asserts Mary is "immortal to the present time through him who had his abode in her and who assumed and raised her above the higher regions."[60]

St. Epiphanius (360):

> Like the bodies of the saints, however, she has been held in honor for her character and understanding. And if I should say anything more in her praise, she is like Elijah, who was virgin from his mother's womb, always remained so, and was taken up, but has not seen death.[61]

St. Gregory of Tours (590):

> And behold, again the Lord stood by them; and the holy body having been received, He commanded that it be taken in a cloud into paradise; where now, rejoined to the soul, [Mary] rejoices with the Lord's chosen ones and is in the enjoyment of the good of an eternity that will never end.[62]

Co-redemptrix and Mediatrix

As stated above, the Fathers of the Church are unanimous when it comes to Mary as "the New Eve." The majority of the references to Mary with this title refer explicitly to her unique role in God's plan of salvation. St. Irenaeus is an excellent example of what we find peppered throughout the age of the Fathers:

> Eve . . . having become disobedient, was made the cause of death, both to herself and to the entire

human race; so also did Mary . . . by yielding obedience, became the cause of salvation, both to herself and the whole human race.[63]

17. Does the bible condemn praying to Mary?

Protestant apologist James White claims praying to Mary and the saints is contrary to Scripture:

> The Bible strongly condemns communication with the dead. It does not matter if those who died were good or bad, saintly or evil, there is to be no communication between the living and the dead. The only communication with spirit beings that originates with man that is allowed in Scripture is that of prayer to God and he alone.[64]

In fact, it is *necromancy*—the conjuring up of the dead through wizards, mediums, etc.—that is condemned in the Bible, not praying to saints.[65] The Church has always condemned necromancy as a grave sin.[66] Mediums, for example, attempt to conjure up spirits and manipulate the spiritual realm at will. This is categorically different from Christians asking for the intercession of Mary and the saints. We do not "conjure up" or manipulate anyone. True prayer—whether to God, the angels, or the saints—changes the pray-er, not the pray-ee.

If one says recklessly, as White does, that "there is to be no communication between the living and the dead," where does this leave Jesus? He is clearly guilty of this, according to Luke 9:29–31:

And as [Jesus] was praying, the appearance of his countenance was altered, and his raiment became dazzling white. And behold, two men talked with him, Moses and Elijah, who appeared in glory and spoke of his departure, which he was to accomplish at Jerusalem.

According to Deuteronomy 34:5, Moses was dead. And yet Jesus was communicating with him and Elijah about the most important event in human history—the redemption.

There is another point to White's argument that requires a deeper level of response. Notice, he said, "The only communication with spirit beings *that originates with man* that is allowed in Scripture is that of prayer to God and he alone."

In one sense, it seems that White—and those who agree with him—is stuck in an Old Testament mindset. We do not see the Old Covenant faithful initiating prayer to the dearly departed, but this is to be expected because the faithful dead before Christ and the beatific vision afforded by him would not have had the power either to hear or to respond to those prayers. Moreover, the Old Covenant People of God did not have the developed understanding of the afterlife that came only with the revelation of Christ.

Jesus Christ clearly introduces a new and radical revelation when he initiates communication with the faithful departed. Even Eric Svendsen seems to understand this when he writes, "The transfiguration was an apocalyptic event choreographed directly by the Son of God to give the apostles a glimpse of his eschatological glory."

If Jesus "choreographed" it, then he *initiated* it. Some may say, "Well, he's God, so he can do that." Yes, he is. But he is also fully man and we are called to imitate him. This is precisely what we mean as Catholics when we say we "pray to Mary and the saints."

Beginning in Hebrews 12:18, the inspired author of that letter encourages the New Covenant faithful by reminding them that their covenant—*the New Covenant*—is far superior to the Old:

> For you have not come to what may be touched, a blazing fire . . . darkness . . . gloom . . . and the sound of a trumpet, and a voice whose words made the hearers entreat that no further messages be spoken to them . . .
>
> But you have come to . . . the city of the living God . . . and to innumerable angels . . . and to the assembly of the first-born who are enrolled in heaven . . . and to . . . God . . . and to the spirits of just men made perfect . . . and to Jesus.

In the Old Covenant, the faithful approached God alone and with trepidation. In the New Covenant: "But you have come to . . . and to . . . and to . . . and to." In the same way we can initiate prayer and in so doing "come to" God and Jesus, we can also "come to" the angels and "the spirits of just men made perfect." That would include Mary and the saints.

The book of Revelation gives us an even better description of this communication between heaven and earth:

> The twenty-four elders fell down before the Lamb, each holding a harp, and with golden bowls full of incense, which are the prayers of the saints . . . the elders fell down and worshipped (5:8–14).

These "elders" are offering the prayers of the faithful symbolized by incense filtering upward from the earth to heaven. And because they are seen receiving these prayers, we can reasonably conclude they were both directed to these saints in heaven and that they were initiated by the faithful living on earth.

18. But didn't Jesus condemn "repetitive prayers" like the rosary?

In Matthew 6:7, Jesus said:

And in praying do not heap up empty phrases [KJV: *vain repetitions*] as the Gentiles do; for they think that they will be heard for their many words.

Some Protestants point to this verse as proof that Catholic prayers like the rosary, which involves repetition of the Lord's Prayer and the Hail Mary, are anti-biblical.

But Jesus never said we cannot pray in repetition at all. He said, "[D]o not heap up 'empty phrases' [Gr.—*battalagesete*, which means to stammer, babble, prate, or to repeat the same things over and over mindlessly] *as the Gentiles do.*"

Historically, the central purpose behind prayer and sacrifice among the pagans was to appease or "take care of" the gods by naming all of their proper titles and saying all of the right words in order to "move" the gods to act. And there was little real connection to the moral life.

This becomes evident when in the very next verses of Matthew 6, Jesus says:

Do not be like them, for your Father knows what you need before you ask him. Pray then like this: Our Father who art in heaven, Hallowed be thy name. Thy kingdom come. Thy will be done . . .

Jesus gave us a prayer to recite, and yes, in "repetitious" fashion, but it has nothing to do with "moving

God." It has everything to do with God moving us! It's "thy will be done," not "my will be done."

There are other instances of repetitious prayer in Scripture. Consider Revelation 4:8:

> And the four living creatures, each of them with six wings, are full of eyes all round and within, and day and night they never cease to sing, "Holy, holy, holy, is the Lord God Almighty, who was and is and is to come!"

Someone needs to inform these angels, who say the same prayer all day and all night, about "vain repetition!"

Both Jews and Christians have prayed the Psalms for thousands of years. Psalm 136 repeats the words "for his steadfast love endures forever" twenty-six times in twenty-six verses!

Perhaps most importantly, we have Jesus in the Garden of Gethsemane:

> And they went to a place which was called Gethsemane. . . . And he said, "Abba, Father, all things are possible to you; remove this chalice from me; yet not what I will, but what you will." And he came and found them sleeping, and he said to Peter, "Simon, are you asleep? Could you not watch one hour? Watch and pray . . ." And again he went away

and prayed, saying the same words. And again, he came and found them sleeping. . . . And he came a third time, and said to them, "Are you still sleeping?" (Mark 14:32–39).

Our Lord was here praying for hours and *saying the same words.* Is this "vain repetition"?

Surely not. And neither is the rosary about mindless repetition to ensure God will hear us and give us what we want. That would be "vain repetition." We Catholics repeat the prayers of the rosary in order to keep our focus while we meditate upon the most important mysteries of the Faith. Each decade has at its end meditation on a different and central mystery in the life of Jesus Christ for our salvation.

Ironically, when I was a Protestant it was far easier to drift into "vain repetition" when all I prayed were "spontaneous" prayers. My prayers often devolved into petition after petition, and through the years I tended to pray the same way, in the same words, over and over.

I have found prayers such as the rosary to have tremendous spiritual benefit. First, all of the prayers and meditations represented are either from Scripture or from the greatest minds and souls who have ever walked the earth before us. They are theologically correct as well as spiritually rich. They free me from having to think about what I am going to say next, and they allow me to really enter into my prayer, and into God. These prayers challenge me at times because of their spiritual depth while they keep me from reducing God to a cosmic bubble-gum machine. "Give me, give me, give me . . ."

Is there a danger of reducing the rosary to mindless recitation? Yes. But this happens in spite of the prayer, not because of it. In the end, I have found the rosary, and other prayers, devotions, and meditations of the Catholic tradition actually save me from the "vain repetition" that Jesus warns about in the Gospel.

19. How do you know alleged "apparitions" of Mary are of God?

First of all, we have to know that apparitions are possible. This can be easily deduced from the Bible. Moses and Elijah, for example, appeared to Jesus on the Mount of Transfiguration (Mt. Tabor) and "talked with him . . . of his exodus, which he was to accomplish at Jerusalem" (Luke 9:30–31). Thus, apparitions are certainly both possible and biblical.

Second, we have to understand apparitions as "private" revelations. The *Catechism* provides:

Throughout the ages, there have been so-called "private" revelations, some of which have been recognized by the authority of the Church. They do not belong, however, to the deposit of faith. It is not their role to improve or complete Christ's definitive Revelation, but to help live more fully by it in a certain period of history. Guided by the Magisterium of the Church, the *sensus fidelium* knows how to discern and welcome in these revelations whatever constitutes an authentic call of Christ or his saints to the Church (CCC 67).

"Public revelation" refers to the "once for all" communication of the deposit of faith that occurred 2,000 years ago through Sacred Scripture and Sacred Tradition.[67] Nothing and no one can add to that sacred deposit. However, the Church will further penetrate into and understand more deeply that revelation until the end of time. This deepening of understanding is the task of the entire people of God, guided by the Magisterium of the Church. Apparitions have a part to play here. Authentic apparitions are gifts from God that serve to enliven our faith and deepen our understanding.

Some private revelations—and apparitions in particular—have been accepted by the Church as worthy of pious belief, or as Pope Benedict XIV said, "human" belief.[68] (But they can never be an object of faith necessary for salvation.) How does the Church discern them?

When an apparition occurs at the outset, the faithful must equip themselves with the *sensus fidelium* that the *Catechism* mentioned above, which guards and guides them in discerning truth from error. But especially when an apparition begins to gain some level of credence in a given locality, the local bishop will often intervene. The local bishop is the ordinary authority to whom the faithful must give religious assent, understanding that the final arbiter, if he so chooses to intervene, is the pope.

Whether on the local or universal level, the Church basically looks for four main criteria in discerning the truth of an apparition.

1. Is there anything in the messages that is contrary to the Faith? If the source is truly the "apparition," errors in faith and morals are a sure sign the apparition is not of God.

2. Are the seers psychologically sound and exemplary in piety, faith, and morals?

3. Is there disobedience to proper authority either not censured or even encouraged by the alleged seers or the "apparition"? Even if there is disagreement with the bishop in matters of prudence, disobedience to his lawful authority is another sure sign that heaven is not involved.

4. As Jesus said plainly in Matthew 7:16: "You shall know them by their fruits."

In a sense, this fourth category covers them all and more. Are people coming back to Christ in his Church through these apparitions? Is there a genuine docility to Christ? Is the authority of the Church being manifested? Are the alleged seers genuine examples of Catholic piety? Are there genuine miracles that cannot be explained by created nature? This last is an exemplary sign that heaven is the true source of the apparition.

Having examined the facts of the case, the Church may (or may not) then decide one of three possibilities:

1. *Constat de supernaturalitate* ("established as supernatural"): This means the Church, either at the local or universal level, has decided this apparition to be worthy of pious belief.

2. *Constat de non supernaturalitate* ("established as not supernatural"): Whether due to a lack of evidence of anything miraculous having occurred (the "apparition" in that case may be the result of overzealous human effort), or due to evidence of the activity of the demonic, this is a clear declaration of the Church that said apparition is not worthy of pious belief.

3. *Non constat de supernaturalitate* ("not established as supernatural"): This judgment says the Church

sees nothing convincing as to its divine origin but is open to further evidence to prove the case.

This process of discernment often takes years. You can rest assured that if the Church does then declare an apparition "worthy of pious belief," you are standing on firm ground in believing the apparition to be true.

20. Why do I need to have a relationship with Mary?

Devotion to Mary is not optional for Christians. As the *Catechism* puts it:

All generations will call me blessed: The Church's devotion to the Blessed Virgin is intrinsic to Christian worship. The Church rightly honors the Blessed Virgin with special devotion. From the most ancient times the Blessed Virgin has been honored with the title of "Mother of God," to whose protection the faithful fly in all their dangers and needs. . . . This very special devotion . . . differs essentially from the adoration which is given to the incarnate Word and equally to the Father and the Holy Spirit, and greatly fosters this adoration (CCC 971).

There are three essential reasons why devotion to Mary is "intrinsic to Christian worship":

1. It is first rooted in the Fourth Commandment: "Honor your father and mother." Because parents uniquely cooperate with God in bringing each new human person into the world, children are obliged to honor, respect, and—as long as they are under their authority—obey their parents in the Lord. This obligation is a matter of justice.

   The devotion we owe to the Blessed Virgin Mary is of a higher order than the honor we give to our parents because Mary's cooperation brings not just biological life, but *eternal life* to "her offspring . . . those who keep the commandments of God and bear testimony to Jesus" (Rev. 12:17). *Gratitude* as well as the virtue of piety (not to mention charity) binds all Christians to offer back to Mary their thanks by way of devotion to her, for all she has done for them.

   Sirach 7:27–28 should be a reminder for us of our duty to respect and honor both our physical parents and our spiritual mother Mary:

   > With all your heart honor your father, and do not forget the birth pangs of your mother. Remember that through your parents you were born; and what can you give back to them that equals their gift to you?

2. Devotion to Mary is rooted in the wondrous interaction, as well as the profound co-dependence, of

the members of the body of Christ. St. Paul captures this reality concisely and beautifully in the image of "the body":

> The eye cannot say to the hand, "I have no need of you," nor again the head to the feet, "I have no need of you." On the contrary . . ." (1 Cor. 12:21).

To say the members of Christ's body are not dependent upon each other for salvation is like saying my finger does not need the rest of my hand for sustenance. God designed the body that way. So it is with the body of Christ. Paul says:

> What then is Apollos? What is Paul? Servants through whom you believed as the Lord assigned to each. . . . For we are God's fellow workers, you are God's field, God's building (1 Cor. 3:5–9).

In bringing Christ to the world and all of her children to Christ, Mary is the example par excellence of just how profoundly members of Christ need one another. We need Mary most of all for the simple reason that *everybody needs a mother.*[69]

3. Out of respect for Mary's office (as *Mother of God*) as well as her holiness, we are called to honor her. Let's first consider special offices in the Church:

But we beseech you, brethren, to respect those who labor among you and are over you in the Lord and admonish you, and to esteem them very highly in love because of their work (1 Thess. 5:12–13).

And then there is the most important reason— *personal holiness.* True greatness in the body of Christ comes through obedience to the word of God.

Whoever then relaxes one of the least of these commandments and teaches men so, shall be called least in the kingdom of heaven; but he who does them and teaches them shall be called great in the kingdom of heaven. For I tell you, unless your righteousness exceeds that of the scribes and Pharisees, you will never enter the kingdom of heaven (Matt. 5:19–20).

Recognizing that she was called to the very highest calling of any human person in history and revealed to be the exemplar of the true disciple—"let it be done unto me according to thy word"—the Church can only echo the divinely inspired words recorded by St. Luke from the lips of our Lady herself:

And Mary said, "My soul magnifies the Lord, and my spirit rejoices in God my Savior, for he

has regarded the low estate of his handmaid-
en. For behold, henceforth all generations will
call me blessed; for he who is mighty has done
great things for me, and holy is his name" (Luke
1:46–49).

Psalm 45:17, which may well be the Old Testament
text behind the words of our Lady, offers a final
insight:

I will cause your name to be celebrated in all
generations; therefore the peoples will praise you
forever and ever.

If you *don't* have a relationship with Mary, the
real question is: *why not?*

About the Author

Tim Staples came from a Fundamentalist background.
During his final year in the United States Marine
Corps, he met a knowledgeable Marine who challenged him to study Catholicism from Catholic and
historical sources. Tim was determined to prove Catholicism wrong. After his tour of duty, he enrolled
at Jimmy Swaggart Bible College and became a youth
minister in an Assemblies of God community. But in
attempting to refute Catholic beliefs, he studied his

way to the last place he thought he would ever end up: the Catholic Church. Tim has given talks in the U.S. and abroad and has helped countless people find their way home to the Church. His extensive knowledge of Scripture makes him without rival in his ability to help others see the strong biblical evidence for Catholic doctrines.

Endnotes

1   Romans 1:3 tells us Christ "was descended from David according to the flesh," which would mean Mary would have descended from David. And the fact that Mary and Joseph offered the offering of the poor at the Presentation in Luke 2:24 (cf. Lev. 12:2–8) indicates Mary to have been poor.

2   According to the second-century document *The Protoevangelium of James*, Mary was 14 to 17 years old when she conceived Jesus. There is a discrepancy in the manuscripts, with variants reading all four ages.

3   Pope Pius IX, *Ineffabilis Deus*, December. 8, 1854.

4   Pope John Paul II, *Redemptoris Mater*, 8.3; 9.1; Rev. R. Ginns, O.P., and Dom Bernard Orchard, O.S.B., eds., *A Catholic Commentary on Sacred Scripture* (New York: Thomas Nelson & Sons, 1953), p. 748.

5   Cf. John 19:3; Acts 23:26.

6   See Gen. 17:5, 15; 32:28; Exod. 3:14.

7   St. Jerome translated *kekaritomene* into Latin as *gratia plena*, or "full of grace," to get at that sense of Mary being *completed* in grace, which is what the *perfect tense* in Greek tends to indicate.

8   In his encyclical *Divinum Illud Munus,* Pope Leo XIII wrote, "Unite, then, venerable brethren, your prayers with ours, and at your exhortation let all Christian peoples add their prayers also, invoking the powerful and ever-acceptable intercession of the Blessed Virgin. You know well the intimate and wonderful relations existing between her and the Holy Ghost, so that she is justly called his spouse."

9   "What then is Apollos? What is Paul? Servants through whom you believed, as the Lord assigned to each. I planted, Apollos watered,

but God gave the growth.... For we are God's *fellow workers*; you are God's field." "Fellow workers" is *sunergoi*, or "co-laborers," in Greek.

10 Cf. James 5:19–20; 1 Tim. 4:16; 1 Cor. 9:22; Rom. 11:14; 1 Cor. 7:16; Col. 1:24; 2 Cor. 1:6; etc.

11 St. Irenaeus, *Against Heresies*, bk. 3, chap. 22, 4.

12 Fr. William Leonard, Dom Bernard Orchard, O.S.B., ed., *A Catholic Commentary on Sacred Scripture* (New York: Thomas Nelson & Sons, 1953), p. 984.

13 "Many" and "all" are, at times, used synonymously in the New Testament, e.g., Rom. 5:18–19.

14 The Greek text here reads *ek pollon kardion dialogismoi*—"the thoughts out of many hearts" may be revealed. The Greek word for "thoughts" is where we get the word *dialogue*. The suffering of Christ on the cross pierces the soul of every man and reveals the innermost "dialogue" of the heart. It is in that "dialogue of the heart" where souls are purified and transformed by grace. Mary's suffering with Christ uniquely participates in both the suffering of Christ and the resulting redemption.

15 Pope Pius XII, *Ad Caeli Reginam*, 34.

16 See also 2 Chron. 15:16; Jer. 13:18.

17 Cf. Eccles. 12:7.

18 CCC 404.

19 Romans 9:11 says that Jacob and Esau, after they were conceived but before they were born, "had done nothing either good or bad."

20 Some may argue that the multiplication of "exceptions" ends up eliminating the norm. This is not so. The general norm of "all have sinned" applies to every human person over the age of accountability (around age 7) except for those who do not have use of their intellects

and wills, and Jesus and Mary. This is hardly a danger to the norm.

21 Eric Svendsen, *Evangelical Answers: A Critique of Current Roman Catholic Apologists* (Lindenhurst, N.Y.: Reformation Press, 1999), p. 137.

22 Rev. S. Shearer, "The 'Brethren of the Lord,'" in *A Catholic Commentary on Sacred Scripture*, p. 844.

23 Some will claim that Mary is *Miriam* in Greek while her sister is *Maria*. However, in Scripture, the two spellings are actually used interchangeably, as we see in the case of Mary Magdalene in Mark 15:40 (she is called "Maria"); Matt. 27:56 ("Maria"), 27:61 ("Mariam"), and 28:1 ("Mariam"). They are essentially the same name.

24 Svendsen, *Evangelical Answers*, 137. Galatians 1:19 is one among a list of seven texts that Svendsen uses to "prove" Mary gave birth to other children through conjugal relations with St. Joseph.

25 The Greek word *apostolos* means "sent one" or "emissary" (CCC 858). Some will include, for example, Andronicus and Junias as apostles in this sense in Romans 16:7. The text is unclear. It says they were "of note among the apostles," not necessarily that they were apostles. But Barnabas is clearly referred to as an apostle, along with St. Paul in Acts 14:14. Moreover, 1 Corinthians 15:5–7 lists *the twelve* and *the apostles* as two distinct categories, indicating there were apostles beyond the twelve. See also 1 Thess. 1:1, 2:6.

26 Cf. Faculty of Theology of the University of Navarre, *The Navarre Bible: The Acts of the Apostles* (Dublin: Four Courts Press, 1992), p. 107.

27 See Acts 8:1.

28 There is no record in Scripture of an *apostle* in an extended sense— beyond the twelve—called such *before* St. Paul was called to be an apostle. Barnabas was the closest to this. He was called, sent, and

referred to as an apostle at about the same time St. Paul was called (see Acts 14:14). Again, it would be unlikely that Paul would be referring to anyone other than the twelve when he refers to apostles who were "before him."

29 Rev. Dom B. Orchard, *A Catholic Commentary on Sacred Scripture*, p. 1115. This well-respected biblical scholar agrees that this visit was a visit to "the twelve" and that among them he saw only Peter and James. St. Jerome, *The Perpetual Virginity of Mary—Against Helvidius*, 15, concurs.

30 In *The Perpetual Virginity of Mary,* 14, St. Jerome adds: "James is called 'the less' (cf. Mark 15:40) in order to distinguish him from James the Greater, who was the son of Zebedee" among the twelve. This is more evidence that the James who is called "the brother of the Lord" was one of the twelve apostles.

31 Svendsen, *Evangelical Answers*, p. 144.

32 Dave Hunt, *A Woman Rides the Beast—The Roman Catholic Church and the Last Days* (Eugene, Ore.: Harvest House Publishers, 1994), p. 436.

33 St. Jerome, *On the Perpetual Virginity of Blessed Mary,* 6.

34 Norman Geisler and Ralph MacKenzie, *Roman Catholics and Evangelicals—Agreements and Differences* (Grand Rapids, Mich.: Baker Books, 1995), p. 322.

35 See Raymond Brown, S.S.; Joseph Fitzmeyer, S.J.; Roland E. Murphy, eds., *The Jerome Biblical Commentary* (Englewood Cliffs, N.J.: Prentice-Hall, 1968), p. 310.

36 See CCC 2110–2114; *Lumen Gentium* 66–67; CCC 971.

37 Cf. Matt. 16:18–19; Luke 22:29–32; 2 Kings 11:1–4; 2 Chron. 15:16; Jer. 13:18; 1 Kings 2:13–23; Luke 1:43; Rev. 12:1–2, 5, etc.

38 Eric Svendsen, *Evangelical Answers*, pp. 156–157.

39 Ibid., p. 157.

40 Cf. St. Thomas Aquinas, *Summa Theologica*, I, q. 12, art. 7.

41 St. Augustine, *On Grace and Free Will*, 31.

42 Revelation 2:10 makes clear that the Christian must "be faithful unto death," and only then will Christ "give [him] the crown of life." Matthew 10:22 says, "[Y]ou will be hated by all for my name's sake. But he who endures to the end will be saved."

43 See also 2 Tim. 2:21; Luke 7:50.

44 Martin Luther, *The Bondage of the Will*, trans. J.I. Packer and O.R. Johnston (Grand Rapids, Mich.: Fleming H. Revell, 1957), p. 294.

45 See Gal. 2:18; 5:1–7.

46 Romans 3:28, 4:5, and Galatians 2:16 speak of "works" done *apart* from Christ being unable to contribute to salvation. Ephesians 2:8–9 speaks of works done *before* entering into Christ being unable to save. But Philippians 4:13 says, "I can do all things in Christ who strengthens me."

47 CCC 2010–2011.

48 See also Matt. 5:44–45; 10:22, 32–33; 12:36–37; 24:44–51; 25:31–46; Eph. 5:3–6; 1 Cor. 6:9–11; 2 Cor. 7:10; Rom. 2:13–16; 6:16; 10:9–10; Heb. 10:26–38; 12:10–16; etc.

49 See also CCC 2007–2010 and CCC 970 for Mary's role in particular.

50 See also Rom. 11:13–14; 1 Cor. 7:16; James 5:19–20; Rev. 19:7–9; Col. 1:24; 2 Cor. 1:6.

51 St. Ignatius of Antioch, *Letter to the Ephesians*, 18, 2.

52 *Against Heresies*, bk. 5, chap. 19, par. 1, cited in William Jurgens, *The Faith of the Early Fathers* (Collegeville, Minn.: Liturgical Press, 1979), vol. 1, p. 101.

53 Cited in Luigi Gambero, *Mary and the Fathers of the Church* (San Francisco: Ignatius Press, 1999), 69–70, 79. See also Origen, *Commentary on Romans*, I, 1, 5 (A.D. 246); Alexander of Alexandria, *Letter to Another Bishop Alexander and All Non-Egyptian Bishops*, 12 (A.D. 324); St. Athanasius, *On the Incarnation of the Word of God*, 8 (A.D. 365). St. Epiphanius, *The Man Well-Anchored*, 75 (A.D. 374). St. Gregory Nazianzen, *Letter 101* (A.D. 382), etc.

54 We do not know who *Mathetes* actually was. There are different theories. The name means "disciple" in Greek and has been attributed to this unknown second-century Christian author.

55 St. Ephrem of Syria, *Op. syr.* II, 37, quoted in Ludwig Ott, *Fundamentals of Catholic Dogma* (Rockford, Ill.: TAN Books and Publishers, 1952), p. 201. See also St. Justin Martyr, *Dialogue with Trypho the Jew*, 100 (A.D. 150); Tertullian, *On the Flesh of Christ*, 17, 5 (A.D. 210); St. Cyril of Jerusalem, *Catechetical Lectures*, Lecture 12, par. 15 (A.D. 350); St. Epiphanius, *Panarion*, 78, 18 (A.D. 360); St. Ephrem of Syria, *Diatesseron*, 10, 13 (A.D. 360); St. John Chrysostom, *Commentary on Psalms*, 44, 7 (A.D. 390), etc.

56 Johannes Quasten, *Patrology* (Allen, Tex.: Christian Classics, 1986), vol. 1, 120–121.

57 *The Instructor*, bk. I, chap. 6.

58 *Commentary on John*, bk. I, chap. 6. See also Eusebius of Caesarea, *Ecclesiastical History*, bk. 2, chap. 1, pars. 2–5 (A.D. 350); St. Athanasius, *Discourse Against the Arians*, 2, 70 (A.D. 356); St. Epiphanius, *Panarion* 11, 5 (A.D. 360); Pope St. Siricius, *Letter to Bishop Anysius* (A.D. 392); St. Ambrose, *Letters,* 11, 5 (A.D. 396); St. Augustine, *On Holy Virginity*, 4, 4 (A.D. 401), etc.

59 Michael O'Carroll, *Theotokos—An Encyclopedia of the Blessed Vir-*

gin Mary (Collegeville, Minn.: Liturgical Press, 1982), p. 59. Critics will say, "Yes, but these are Gnostic works." And that is true. But in the volume upon volume of Christian works against the false doctrines of Gnosticism, we never have a single condemnation of this particular teaching. As we'll see below, we see just the opposite.

60 Quoted in ibid., 388. The author states that there is disagreement among scholars as to the dating of this homily. "Fr. M. Jugie, A.A., opting for the fourth century against Dom Bernard Capelle, O.S.B., an eminent liturgical historian, who defends the sixth or seventh centuries as the probable time."

61 St. Epiphanius, *Panarion* 79: 5, 1. The Church has never defined infallibly whether Mary died or not before being assumed into heaven, though at the level of the Ordinary Magisterium, the Church does teach that Mary died. See, for example, Pope Pius XII, *Munificentissimus Deus*, 17, 20, 21, 29, 35, 39, and 40.

62 Jurgens, vol. 3, 306. See also Theodosius of Alexandria, *On the Dormition of Mary*, 5 (567); Theoteknos, Bishop of Livias, Homily, "On the Dormition," (625); St. Germanus of Constantinople, Homily 1, "On the Most Venerable Dormition of the Holy Mother of God" (733); St. Andrew of Crete, Homily, "On the Dormition of our Most Holy Lady, Mother of God" (740); St. John Damascene, Homily III, "On the Dormition of Our Lady" (750).

63 St. Irenaeus, *Against Heresies*, bk. 3, chap. 22, 4. See Michael O'Carroll's *Theotokos—An Encyclopedia of the Blessed Virgin Mary* for more examples of Mary as "the New Eve."

64 James White, *Answer to Catholic Claims—A Discussion of Biblical Authority* (Southbridge, Mass.: Crowne Publications, Inc., 1990), p. 126.

65 See Deut. 18:10–11; Isa. 19:3.

66 CCC 2116–2117.

67 See Jude 3.

68 Benedict XIV, *De Serv. Dei Beatif. et Beat. Canonizatione.*

69 The fact that Jesus gave his mother to all of us from the cross in John 19:25–26 is a powerful example of just how much Jesus knew that we needed a spiritual mother in our lives (see also Rev. 12:17).

Become part of the team.
Help support Catholic Answers.

Catholic Answers is an apostolate dedicated to serving Christ by bringing the fullness of Catholic truth to the world. We help good Catholics become better Catholics, bring former Catholics "home," and lead non-Catholics into the fullness of the Faith.

Catholic Answers neither asks for nor receives financial support from any diocese. The majority of its annual income is in the form of donations from individual supporters like you.

To make a donation by phone using your credit card, please speak with one of our customer service representatives at 888-291-8000.

To make a donation by check, please send a check payable to "Catholic Answers" to:

Catholic Answers
2020 Gillespie Way
El Cajon, CA 92020

To make a donation online, visit **catholic.com**.

TO EXPLAIN & DEFEND THE FAITH

catholic.com